CEZANNE
THE STEINS
AND
THEIR CIRCLE

THIS IS THE EIGHTEENTH OF THE
WALTER NEURATH MEMORIAL LECTURES
WHICH ARE GIVEN ANNUALLY EACH SPRING ON
SUBJECTS REFLECTING THE INTERESTS OF
THE FOUNDER
OF THAMES AND HUDSON

THE DIRECTORS WISH TO EXPRESS
PARTICULAR GRATITUDE TO THE GOVERNORS AND
MASTER OF BIRKBECK COLLEGE
UNIVERSITY OF LONDON
FOR THEIR GRACIOUS SPONSORSHIP OF
THESE LECTURES

CEZANNE
THE STEINS
AND
THEIR CIRCLE

JOHN REWALD

THAMES AND HUDSON

The text of this lecture has been condensed from two chapters of an A. W. Mellon
lecture series which will be published by Princeton University Press and Thames and Hudson
in 1987 under the title Cézanne and America

First published in the USA in 1987 by Thames and Hudson Inc.,
500 Fifth Avenue, New York, New York 10110

Library of Congress Catalog Card Number 86–50805

Printed and bound in Great Britain

I met Walter Neurath only once and never really dealt with him as a publisher, yet I have the deepest respect for him just as much for what he did as for what he left behind. Indeed, the publishing house which he established, and which continues to follow the splendid example he set, has my total admiration. It is rare to collaborate with publishers who care for their authors, encourage them, show them constant consideration, present their manuscripts in beautiful volumes ... and even flatter them. That, I am convinced, is a tradition established by Walter Neurath, and I, for one, enjoy and am grateful for every minute of it.

1 Leo, Gertrude and Michael Stein in the courtyard of their rue de Fleurus apartment, early 1906

MICHAEL, LEO and GERTRUDE STEIN, born in Pittsburgh, Pennsylvania – Michael in 1865, Leo in 1872 and Gertrude in 1874 – were brought by their father, who was a wealthy middle-class merchant, to Europe early in life. Gertrude was to write to a friend, 'I guess you know my life history well enough, that I was in Vienna from six months of age to four years, that I was in Paris from 4 years of age to 5, that I was in Cal[ifornia] from six years of age to seventeen.'[1] Their father died in Oakland, California, in 1891, and Michael Stein became head of the family at the age of 26. The following year Leo, who was 20, went to Harvard, and in 1893 Gertrude, aged 19, was enrolled at Radcliffe. In 1896 Leo and Gertrude entered John Hopkins University in Baltimore, Leo to study biology, Gertrude medicine. Four years later Leo settled in Florence, intending to write a book on Mantegna. There his interests crystalized in aesthetics, partly under the influence of the art historian Bernard Berenson, with whom he developed a friendship that was to last for the next four decades. He remained in Florence for two years. In 1902 Gertrude joined him in London for six months, while Berenson too was there, but they found London depressing.

Leo left London for Paris in 1902, planning to go to America, where Gertrude had already returned.

But one night in Paris when he was dining with Pablo Casals, as he often did, and expounding on his theories of aesthetics, he suddenly felt himself 'growing into an artist'. He went back to his hotel, made a fire, took off his clothes, and began to draw from the nude. He spent the next week drawing from statues in the Louvre, then began painting at the Académie Julian. A sculptor cousin recently arrived in Paris had just found a place to live; 'as I don't like apartment hunting, I said to him that doubtless he had taken the best he found: what was the next best? He said the next best was 27 rue de Fleurus. So I settled at 27 rue de Fleurus.'[2]

Gertrude joined him there in 1903.

7

2 *The Conduit, c.*1879

3 *Montagne Sainte-Victoire and Village near Gardanne*, 1886–90

Early in 1904 Leo Stein asked Berenson whether there were any living artists in France deserving attention. 'Do you know Cézanne?' asked Berenson. 'No', said Leo. 'Well, look him up.' – 'Where?' – 'At Vollard's on the Rue Lafitte.'[3] Whereupon the neophyte collector acquired a landscape from Vollard. That summer Stein went as usual to Florence where he spent more time with Cézanne than he did with the pictures in the Uffizi and the Pitti. This happened after Berenson told him that an American expatriate, Charles Loeser, his Florentine neighbour, owned many of the artist's works. Leo was later to write of Loeser that 'he had begun buying Cézannes in the early days, when Vollard's was a kind of five-and-ten establishment, and had got together an interesting lot.... When I got back to Paris after the Cézanne debauch, I was ready to look further.'[4]

4 Madame Cézanne with a Fan, 1886–88

5 *Five Apples*, 1877–78

Looking further, Leo visited Vollard for new purchases to succeed the landscape acquired earlier that year. That landscape of rippling greens and full of light shows a fascinating juxtaposition of verticals, horizontals, and a few discreet diagonals; its brushwork is free and incisive. Towards the end of 1904 Gertrude informed a friend, 'We is doin business too we are selling Jap prints to buy a Cezanne at least we are that is Leo is trying. He don't like it a bit and makes a awful fuss about asking enough money but I guess we'll get the Cezanne.'[5] That picture was doubtless the portrait of the artist's wife shown at the Salon d'Automne of 1904.   4

No complete list of Cézanne's works owned by Leo and Gertrude Stein seems ever to have been established,[6] nor are the dates known at which most of them were acquired, but among the oils and watercolours they assembled, this portrait of the artist's wife was, in addition to the landscape, the most important Cézanne in their collection. It was the only picture at the Steins that Fernande Olivier, Picasso's mistress, specifically remembered, for she spoke later of 'that beautiful likeness of the painter's wife in a blue dress, sitting in a garnet-coloured armchair.'[7] There were also two medium-sized compositions of bathers, purchased   10, 11 from Vollard, a small still-life of powerfully modelled apples, and a   5 study of a man with a pipe. There were at least five watercolours, of   6

6 Man with Pipe, 1892–96

which one of a smoking peasant was probably the most remarkable; the 7
others were landscapes, among them two views of Montagne Sainte- 8, 9
Victoire. Yet there may have been more; Fernande Olivier mentioned 'a
large quantity of watercolours by Cézanne, bathers in landscape settings,
etc.' Vollard held his first exhibition of the artist's watercolours in 1905
and it appears likely that the Steins' first purchases of watercolours date
from that show.

7 *The Smoker,*
1890–91

8 *Montagne Sainte-Victoire*, c.1890

9 *Montagne Sainte-Victoire*, 1900–02

10 *Bathers*, 1898–1900

11 *Group of Bathers*, 1892–94

Leo and Gertrude's brother Michael and his wife Sally, who then also lived in Paris, had at least one painting by Cézanne, a tiny *Portrait of* 12 *the Artist's Son.* An exquisitely delicate work of thin, transparent glazes that seem to touch the surface only lightly, with part of the bare canvas showing, it is nevertheless fully resolved as a tender statement.

However, Michael and Sally Stein's collection was almost ex- 13 clusively geared to Matisse, with whom they maintained close and warm ties,[8] while Leo and Gertrude played an important role in the dissemination, not only of Matisse's fame, but that of Cézanne and Picasso as well. Their house was virtually open, in particular to any fellow countryman passing through or living in Paris, and to many others too, such as the English critics Roger Fry, Clive Bell, C. Lewis Hind and Frank Rutter, or such Russian fellow collectors as Sergei Shchukin and Ivan Morosov.[9] Leo and Gertrude owned more works

13 Michael and Sally Stein's apartment, 58 rue Madame, showing part of their collection of works by Matisse, c.1908. These include *The Gypsy*, 1906 (top left), a study for *Bonheur de vivre*, 1905, now in a private collection (second row from left, centre); *Madame Matisse* ('*The Green Line*'), 1905, now in the Statens Museum for Kunst, Copenhagen (second row from left, bottom); *The Young Sailor I*, 1906 (third row from left, top); below it, *Blue Still-life*, 1907, now owned by the Barnes Foundation, Merion, Pennsylvania; *Self-portrait*, 1906, now in the Statens Museum for Kunst, Copenhagen (right-hand row, top); and *Woman with a Branch of Ivy* (*L'Italienne*), c.1905 (right-hand row, bottom).

14 Leo and Gertrude's apartment in the rue de Fleurus with, among other works, Cézanne's portrait of Madame Cézanne, now owned by the Emil G. Bührle Foundation, Zürich (see no. 4), to its left a Japanese scroll and, on the right-hand wall, Matisse's *Woman with a Hat* of 1904–05, now in a private collection

14, 15   by Cézanne than could be seen at the Musée du Luxembourg — then the major French collection of modern art — not to mention the watercolours, of which the Luxembourg had none. Hardly any American artist or writer who went to Paris, which was becoming increasingly popular among the international avant-garde, failed to visit them or remained indifferent to the accumulation of paintings on the
16–19   cluttered walls of their rue de Fleurus apartment.

    Typical of the way in which collectors can influence their contemporaries, Leo, having been encouraged by the example of Charles Loeser, in turn transmitted his appetite to others. It seems, for example, that Albert Barnes owed his introduction to Cézanne to the Steins. At least it can be said that Barnes' preferences show remarkable parallels to those of Leo. His vast collection was to be built around the two artists who were Leo's favourites, Renoir and Cézanne. To these he added, among the younger masters, especially Matisse, a knowledge of whom he always connected with Leo Stein.

In the beginning, not all the visitors to the Steins shared their tastes in art. During the summer of 1905, when the collection was still in a very early stage, the painter Alfred Maurer and a fellow American, the sculptor Mahonri Young, took visitors to see the pictures while Leo and Gertrude were in Florence. 'Young and I shocked some Americans the other day with them,' Maurer gleefully reported to Leo. 'The lady wanted to know if I was in earnest.'[10] He was, though one could not

15 Leo Stein in his rue de Fleurus apartment, c.1905. Among the paintings are works by Gauguin (second from left), Renoir (above Leo's head), Maurice Denis (*Maternity*) and Cézanne (*Group of Bathers*, now owned by the Barnes Foundation, Merion, Pennsylvania; see no. 11).

16 *Landscape by the Waterside*, 1878–80

always be certain of it, particularly when he discussed the problem of
finish, which was constantly brought up in connection with Cézanne,
whereas it was no longer questioned concerning the other Impressionists.
4 In such instances Maurer would point to the portrait of Madame
Cézanne, declaring 'you could tell it is finished because it has a frame.'[11]

As Mabel Dodge, one of Leo's and Gertrude's intimates, later wrote:
'In those early days when everyone laughed, and went to the Steins' for
the fun of it, and half angrily, half jestingly giggled and scoffed after they
left ... Leo stood patiently night after night wrestling with the inertia of
his guests, expounding, teaching, interpreting. ...' According to Mabel
Dodge, 'buying those distorted compositions and hanging them in his

apartment, Leo felt the need for making others see what he found in them, and this turned him eloquent.'[12] Leo himself spoke of 'the obligation that I have been under ever since the Autumn Salon [of 1904], of expounding L'Art Moderne. ... The men whose pictures we have bought – Renoir, Cézanne, Gauguin, Maurice Denis – and others whose pictures we have not bought but would like to – Manet, Degas, Vuillard, Bonnard, Van Gogh for example – all belong. To make the subject clear requires a discussion of the qualities of the men of '70 of whom the Big Four and Puvis de Chavannes are ... the inspirers in the main of the vital art of today. The Big Four are Manet Renoir Degas & Cézanne.'

17 *Forest Path*, 1882–84

18 *The Coach House at Château Noir*, 1890–95

19 *Olive Grove*, c.1900

20 Leo and Gertrude Stein's apartment, early 1906. Far left, above the sofa, is Cézanne's *The Smoker*, now owned by the Barnes Foundation, Merion, Pennsylvania (see no. 7); the large nude in the centre is Bonnard's *Siesta – The Artist's Studio*, now in the National Gallery of Victoria, Melbourne, and on the right is Picasso's *Young Girl with a Basket of Flowers*, 1905, now in a private collection

21 Paintings by Gauguin (top centre), Matisse (centre and below right), Toulouse-Lautrec (centre, left) and Picasso (top right) in Leo and Gertrude Stein's apartment in the rue de Fleurus

Whereupon Leo would launch into the 'required discussion', saying notably of Cézanne:

here is great mind, a perfect concentration and great control. Cézanne's essential problem is mass and he has succeeded in rendering mass with a vital intensity that is unparalleled in the whole history of painting. No matter what his subject is – the figure – the landscape – still life – there is always this remorseless intensity, this endless unending gripping of the form, the unceasing effort to force it to reveal its absolute self-existing quality of mass. There can scarcely be such a thing as a completed Cézanne. Every canvas is a battlefield and victory an unattainable ideal. Cézanne rarely does more than one thing at a time and when he turns to composition he brings to bear the same intensity, keying his composition up till it sings like a harp string. His colour also, though as harsh as his forms, is almost as vibrant. In brief, his is the most robust, the most intense and, in a fine sense, the most ideal of the four.[13]

But no sooner had Leo established a very special relationship with Cézanne, whose intellect and aims appear to have been closest to his heart (if not his eyes, which liked to feast on Renoir's exuberant colours) than there came the discovery of Matisse in 1905, supplemented quickly by the first purchases of his works and acquaintance with the artist. This was followed shortly by the addition of Picasso to the Stein collection and to their circle of friends. With them grew Leo's 'obligation' to extend his propagandizing efforts on behalf of their work. 'I expounded and explained', Leo subsequently wrote. 'People came, and so I explained, because it was my nature to explain.'[14] In later years Leo also remembered: 'One man who came to my place in Paris told me that the only Cézannes he cared for were those he saw there. Certainly they were not the best Cézannes, but the place was charged with the atmosphere of propaganda and he succumbed.'[15]

Even when discussing other artists, Leo often would finish by referring to Cézanne. In a letter to a friend he began by explaining:

The thing that Matisse has as his dominant character is clarity ... I can't speak of the clarity of his color or form properly, but rather for me his color & form result in a total expression for which clarity is the best term. Michael Angelo & Cézanne are so far as I know the great masters of Volume.... The difference between an apple of Cézanne & a nude of Michael Angelo lies mainly in the complexity of organization.[16]

22 From left to right: Michael and Sally Stein, Henri Matisse, Allan Stein (Michael and Sally's son) and Hans Purrman (a German painter and pupil of Matisse) at Michael and Sally Stein's apartment, 58 rue Madame, c.1908. All the paintings are by Matisse.

When Berenson occasionally dropped in on the Steins, he was probably provoked into verbal jousts with Leo, who must have been happy to elaborate in still greater detail on the analogies between the masters of the Renaissance and Cézanne. It was at the rue de Fleurus that Berenson met Picasso, yet it was Sally Stein who introduced him to Matisse, with whose faculties and principles he was deeply impressed.[17] Whereupon the entire Stein family, as Berenson later said (not too graciously), 'who at that time arrogated to themselves the office of High Protectors of newness in painting, began to prod me to leave all I had and to dedicate myself to expounding the merits of the new school. When I would not, they sadly put me down as having made a great refusal.'[18]

22

Whether Leo had any further discussions with Berenson concerning Cézanne is not known, but Cézanne did remain on Berenson's mind and, in 1910, for example, he was to write from Ravenna to his wife: 'I have never before noticed so clearly the resemblance between the technique of colour in mosaic and in our impressionists as in Cézanne for instance. They have in common a procedure of juxtaposition of tones.'[19] It would have been very surprising had Leo agreed with this rather shallow analogy. In any case, a young American philosopher and friend of Leo, Willard Huntington Wright, would soon 'reply' to Berenson, even though he was certainly not aware of Berenson's observation. Trying to explain Cézanne's aversion to the primitives, in whom he saw but the rudiments of art, Wright stated:

How could Cézanne, preoccupied with the most momentous problems of aesthetics, take an interest in enlarged book illuminations, when the most superficial corner of his slightest canvas had more organisation and incited a greater aesthetic emotion than all the mosaics in S. Vitale at Ravenna?[20]

But if Stein and Berenson no longer found any common ground for communicating on the subject of Cézanne, Leo did continue to discuss the artist with many and more receptive friends, such as, among others, the American painter Morgan Russell who, upon his arrival in Paris in 1908, had passed through an interesting evolution of raptures. At first Russell had been captivated by the paintings of Monet, in whom he saw the 'master of light'. However, in a letter to his friend Andrew Dasburg,

23 Morgan Russell, *Three Apples*, 1910

Russell specified that 'Monet is not the only one: wait till you get acquainted with Gauguin, Cézanne, and the younger men, Matisse, etc. ...'[21] It was Leo Stein who had awakened Russell's interest in Cézanne, and when Russell was joined in Paris by Andrew Dasburg, the two young artists even borrowed the small still-life of apples by Cézanne from Leo and painted works directly inspired by it. 'To me the original is infinitive', Dasburg wrote to his wife. 'It will rest in my mind as a standard of what I want to attain in my paintings. ...'[22]

5
23

Leo continued their discussions even from Fiesole, near Florence, telling Russell in a letter:

I noticed at Rome that nowhere on the ceiling has Michelangelo attained to the sheer expression of form that is often achieved in his drawings. I believe that nowhere is it as complete as in those apples of Cézanne's. Cézanne must for the ... general public always remain a painter of still life because there only could

24 Leo Stein, at the rue de Fleurus apartment, *c.*1906

he 'realize', in the ordinary sense of the word, without sacrificing his aesthetic conscience.[23]

Sometimes, when Leo took a personal interest in the education of a young artist, he would introduce the beginner to Vollard who would bring out half a dozen canvases.[24] Yet not even Leo's intervention could make the dealer depart from his habit of presenting only a few pictures at a time while hundreds of them were literally piled up in his closets. According to the critic Max Raphael, who was in Paris at the time, Vollard felt 'that one should not show good pictures to painters and writers because they then talked and wrote about them, with the result that it became difficult to sell the bad works.'[25]

It is likely that when Leo discussed Cézanne at the Steins' Saturday soirées, he most often spoke of what he considered to be the artist's superior mind, perfect concentration and great control, as well as complexity of organization and sheer expression of form, of fullness, of mass. Eventually, Leo was to put it more succinctly when he wrote that in those early days he had been 'especially obsessed by Cézanne's plastic presentations.'[26] Not until the very twilight of his life was Berenson to express a somewhat similar thought when he compared Piero della Francesca and Cézanne, stating that 'the former is almost as indifferent as the other to what we are accustomed to regard as physical beauty. Both are more aware of bulk and weight than of looks. . . .' But whereas Berenson eventually grasped some of Cézanne's traits, such as his tendency to express 'character, essence rather than momentary feeling or purpose',[27] Leo moved in the opposite direction. Instead of penetrating ever deeper into the mysteries that the painter presented, he became – as time passed – actually less and less erudite in his interpretations.

Whether Leo was too wrapped up in his explanations to listen to what others had to say, the fact is that he neglected to report any remarks provoked by the pictures on which he so endlessly held forth. And his sister did not do any better. In the beginning, according to an old friend of theirs, she had been 'possessed by a singular devotion to Leo; she admired and loved him in a way a man is seldom admired and loved.'[28] But once their close attachment succumbed in the face of Gertrude's

25 (overleaf) Alice Toklas and Gertrude Stein in the rue de Fleurus apartment, 1922, photographed by Man Ray. A painting of bathers by Cézanne hangs immediately above the fireplace on the left and his portrait of Madame Cézanne (see no. 4) appears on the right, above Gertrude. To the left of it is a nude by Picasso

stronger relationship with Alice Toklas, and each withdrew into an almost monstrously self-conscious egotism, Gertrude may have lost interest in what Leo propounded. By the time she got around to writing the *Autobiography of Alice B. Toklas*, in 1933, she had so successfully eliminated Leo from her life – including the years they had spent together – that she could speak of the early days in Paris and of their collection without even alluding to her brother. Thus, she was to write:

... Slowly through all this and looking at many many pictures I came to Cézanne and there you were, at least there I was, not all at once but as soon as I got used to it. The landscape looked like a landscape. ... The same thing was true of the people there was no reason why it should be but it was, the same thing was true of the chairs, the same thing was true of the apples. ... They were so entirely these things that they were not an oil painting and yet that is just what the Cézannes were they were an oil painting. They were so entirely an oil painting that it was all there whether they were finished, the paintings, or whether they were not finished. Finished or unfinished it always was what it looked like the very essence of an oil painting because everything was always there, really there.[29]

Even before Gertrude and Leo split up, she had been a poor listener, which meant that she didn't really care for the opinions of others. As a result, posterity has been deprived of the comments that such visitors to the rue de Fleurus as Matisse or Picasso cannot have failed to make. Matisse, whose intelligence greatly impressed Leo and who himself profoundly admired Cézanne, must have commented on the works accumulated by his hosts, while the more whimsical and not yet very sociable Picasso may have uttered less memorable words.

That Picasso was far from indifferent to the Steins' portrait of 4, 27 Madame Cézanne is shown by his portrait of Gertrude. It was painted during the winter of 1905–06 in Picasso's Montmartre studio rather than in the rue de Fleurus under the very eyes of Madame Cézanne, so to speak. Nevertheless, Madame Cézanne seems to 'hover' over Picasso's image of Gertrude and there are definite analogies between the two paintings. These concern not only the curve of the armchair which in each case separates the sitter from the room that forms the background

26 *(opposite)* Paintings in Leo and Gertrude Stein's apartment: Matisse's *Bonheur de vivre*, 1905–06, now owned by the Barnes Foundation, Merion, Pennsylvania (top), and works by Renoir (the two women and the head of a girl) and Cézanne (the portrait of his wife and a painting of bathers to its left – both reproduced above; nos 4 and 10)

(and the vertical line that appears in both of them), but also the hands, particularly the left ones, the three-quarter angle of the pose, and – above all – the masklike appearance of each face. It is known that, dissatisfied with Gertrude's head as it emerged after many sittings, Picasso wiped it out, only to repaint it while Miss Stein was in Italy, without having his model before him. This accounts for the fact that her features appear so much less naturalistic than the rest of the picture.[30]

It would seem, though this has not been established with certainty, that something similar had occurred in the likeness of Madame Cézanne. The discreet wallpaper of bluish floral sprays in the background of her portrait can be identified with lodgings Cézanne occupied in 1879–80, but the much less volumetric head of the sitter appears to have been painted several years later. Here, too, it looks as though, after an interruption, the artist returned to the canvas to rework some parts, especially the face. Here, too, there is a perceptible hiatus, accented – as in Picasso's painting – by the sharp contour of the head, notably the line that leads from the ear to the chin, as though it were encompassing the area to which the alterations were confined. In both canvases there are also those penetrating yet almost 'empty' and absent eyes that appear to be remembered rather than observed.

When Picasso obliterated Gertrude's face and left it blank, waiting for the moment when a satisfactory solution would occur to him, he obviously was not imitating Cézanne; he probably did not even suspect that Cézanne may have proceeded in the same fashion. But he was too keenly observant not to have noticed the determined outline that sets off Madame Cézanne's face, nor the burning, dark eyes that, in his own painting, look like incisions, comparable to those African masks with which he was beginning to be fascinated. Did Picasso ever speak of Cézanne while Gertrude sat for him? We shall never know; she was thinking of a story she planned to write and even if she paid any attention to what he uttered, she never mentioned it afterwards. The only thing she did say about the picture was that her first book, *Three Lives*, published in 1908, was written under the stimulus of Madame Cézanne's portrait.

It is difficult not to quote here Clive Bell's rather blunt views of the Steins, according to which 'neither, so far as I could make out, had a

27 Pablo Picasso, *Gertrude Stein*, 1906

genuine feeling for visual art.... The truth is that they were a pair of theorists – Leo possessing the better brain and Gertrude the stronger character – and that for them pictures were pegs on which to hang hypotheses.... It was their brother Michael who loved painting.'[31]

The gatherings at the Steins furnished more than opportunities for endless discussions animated by Leo's analytical mind: they were also illustrated by the pictures that the brother and sister (that is, in those days mostly Leo) had assembled. What made the Stein collection so unique was that it provided fascinating juxtapositions of tendencies of the recent past with the latest developments. Cézanne was being increasingly regarded as the dominant figure among the precursors of contemporary art, whereas Monet and Renoir – then both still active – enjoyed less popularity with the young, though Leo Stein was and remained partial to Renoir and owned quite a few of his paintings. But to see Cézanne's works next to recent ones by Matisse and Picasso became a major attraction and offered visitors to the rue de Fleurus a singular initiation into prevalent new trends, extending from Cézanne to Fauvism and, subsequently, Cubism. To many guests of the Steins, Matisse and Picasso appeared almost too overpowering in their daring and unorthodoxy. Next to them, Cézanne assumed the position of a classic, and some younger Frenchmen began to hail him as such. He offered a means to overcome Impressionism, which was only beginning to become popular, but which – for many of the new generation of artists – was already becoming slightly *passé*. To them it was Cézanne who opened the path to new and radical achievements, a path on which Matisse and Picasso were advancing boldly.

When Cubism made its appearance around 1907 and claimed the recently deceased Cézanne among its forefathers, the master's work gained an additional significance. As Gertrude Stein began to acquire Picasso's early Cubist paintings – to which her brother was violently opposed – discussions at the rue de Fleurus might have found themselves further amplified, but the opposite was the case. By 1910, Leo, as he later explained, 'had had enough of intensive concern with so-called modern art.... When my interest in Cézanne declined, when Matisse was temporarily in eclipse, when Picasso turned to foolishness, I began to withdraw from the Saturday evenings.'[32] In the absence of Leo and his stimulating ideas, his rather placid sister began to reign over the rue de Fleurus gatherings. Liberated from the intellectual dominance of her brother, Gertrude now liked to draw parallels between Picasso's Cubism and her own peculiar literary style,[33] but otherwise she did not contribute much to discussions on art.

Whenever she expressed herself on artistic matters, she would – true to herself – use lots of words for saying rather little. One of her pet theories was that paintings have a tendency 'either to remain in their frames or to escape from them.'[34] She also used to explain that for her all modern painting was 'based on that which Cézanne failed to do instead of being based on that which he almost succeeded in doing.'[35]

This was a strangely ungenerous view of the artist and one that totally neglected to mention whatever, in Gertrude's view, he did *not* fail to do, the more so as she would only grant that he had *almost* succeeded in his aims. Though she does not seem to have cared for totally abstract art, it would appear that Gertrude's approach to painting was based on the premise that anything unconventional was attractive. And the more radical it was, the more she liked it. In later years Leo stated more than once that his sister's art appreciation had been neither deep nor original and that her subsequent accounts of her aesthetic discoveries were not truthful. It is nevertheless a fact that she added many Cubist Picassos to the collection.

Although discussions of stylistic problems seem slowly to have slackened at the rue de Fleurus, especially after Leo had moved to Florence in 1914, taking several Cézannes and all the Renoirs with him,[36] the absence of his constant explanations may have done no harm to the reception of the pictures, which were now allowed to speak for themselves. The painters who came to see them were interested more in visual experiences than in listening to lengthy speculations. But with Gertrude not very articulate on questions of art and with Leo hostile to Cubism, it seems doubtful that the Stein circle played a very active part in establishing the Cubist understanding of Cézanne as the orthodox mainstream tradition of that new style.

28 *(overleaf)* Leo and Gertrude Stein's apartment, with Picasso's portrait of Gertrude Stein, two other paintings by him (the large nude on the far left and the small head below it), Matisse's *Woman with a Hat*, 1905, and at its right a landscape by him; and a work by Renoir (the woman in a hat), far right

29 Alfred Maurer, *Still-life*, 1907–08

Alfred Maurer, in any case, proved to be more receptive to Matisse's colours and execution, actually becoming the first American to work in a Fauvist vein. Among the other American artists who visited the Steins were Walter Pach, Stanton Macdonald-Wright (who shortly after arriving in Paris in 1907 acquired four Cézanne watercolours[37]), Patrick Henry Bruce and Edward Steichen, who eventually became a kind of Paris scout for the New York gallery of his friend Alfred Stieglitz, whom he also took to the rue de Fleurus.

30 Alfred Maurer, *Fauve Landscape*

More than any other American of those days, Patrick Henry Bruce seems to have found the key to Cézanne's perceptions. Yet – true artist that he was – he could not be satisfied with mere imitation. Even though he achieved a profoundly painterly expression in the wake of Cézanne, he soon did what every genuine creator must do: he used what his chosen master offered as a stepping-stone towards independent self- 31 fulfilment. Together with Sally Stein, Bruce became instrumental in setting up Matisse's Académie at the Couvent des Oiseaux, opened in

January 1908. There Matisse never tired of proclaiming that Cézanne was 'the father of us all', guiding his students through word and example towards a full grasp of how colour functions to model form in space.[38]

The American Max Weber was also a student at Matisse's Académie, while Leo Stein, Maurice Sterne and Walter Pach dropped in occasionally. According to Weber's recollections, 'a counterpoint and enhancement of the workaday spirit of the class were the occasional visits to Matisse's [own] studio in another part of the Couvent des Oiseaux. . . . With great modesty and deep inner pride, he showed us his painting of *Bathers* by Cézanne. His silence before it was more evocative and eloquent than words. A spirit of elation and awe pervaded the studio at such times.'[39]

Although he was not the only one whose efforts helped create interest and understanding for the master, Matisse performed an extremely

31 Patrick Henry Bruce, *Still-life*, *c.*1921–22

32 *Three Bathers*, 1876–77

important role in the propagandizing of Cézanne's innovations. Through his friendship with Leo and Gertude, as well as with Michael and Sally Stein, Matisse reached a number of young American artists and thus contributed much to spreading Cézanne's 'message' across the Atlantic.[40] 33, 34

In May 1915, Leo Stein returned to the United States for – among other reasons – a second attempt at psychoanalysis, having been dissatisfied with a first one.

33 Morgan Russell, *Still-life with Bananas*, 1912–13

In New York he reestablished contact with his friend Willard
Huntington Wright. He was also in touch with Albert Barnes who was
'still collecting, chiefly Renoirs, of which he has now about sixty.'[41]

Meanwhile, Willard Huntington Wright involved himself in what
was to become famous as the Forum Exhibition, held in 1916, which
was devoted exclusively to American avant-garde painting and was
assembled much more carefully – and kept to a smaller scale – than the
Armory Show had been three years before. For his introductory essay,
Wright simply used the first chapter of his recently published volume,
Modern Painting: Its Tendency and Meaning. Though this was a rather
general text, what he had said there on Cézanne now took on a more

34 Stanton Macdonald-Wright, *Still-life with Skull*, 1912

precise meaning due to the special context, since the exhibition, while
not containing any works by Cézanne, featured a number of important
new Synchromist paintings by Willard's brother S. Macdonald-   35, 36
Wright and other artists. Indeed, Wright hailed Cézanne as the forebear
of the Synchromists – who painted in a brilliant chromatic idiom –
when he summed up the recent artistic evolution as follows:

The Impressionists, being interested in nature as a manifestation in which light
plays the all-important part, transferred it bodily onto canvas.... Cézanne,
looking into their habits more coolly, saw their restrictions. While achieving all
their atmospheric aims, he went deeper into the mechanics of color, and with
this knowledge achieved form as well as light. This was another step forward in

49

the development of modern methods. With him color began to near its true and ultimate significance as a functioning element. Later, with the aid of the scientists Chevreul, Superville, Helmholtz and Rood, other artists made various departures into the field of color, but their enterprises were failures. Then came Matisse, who made improvements on the harmonic side of color. But because he ignored the profounder lessons of Cézanne, he succeeded only in the fabrication of a highly organized decorative art. Not until the advent of the Synchromists ... were any further crucial advances made. The artists completed Cézanne in that they rationalized his dimly foreshadowed precepts.[42]

Though, in connection with this show, Cézanne came to be perceived mainly as a milestone on the road to Synchromism, Wright was careful not to reduce his historic role to that of a mere forerunner of his brother and his friends. At the same time, Wright now began to review exhibitions, notably one of watercolours by Cézanne, whose importance he never tired of stressing.

Shortly after his arrival in New York, and in order to finance his trip as well as his treatment, Leo Stein disposed of his small composition of 10, 5 bathers by Cézanne. All he now had left was the small still-life of apples and a few watercolours by the painter, as well as some works by other artists, especially Renoir. The *Bathers* was acquired by Dr Barnes for $5000.

In a strange parallel, both Leo Stein and Willard Huntington Wright were then immersed in problems of philosophy and aesthetics. They seem to have met frequently in Stieglitz's '291' gallery, where they engaged in extremely animated discussions.[43] Having just published his volume *Modern Painting*, Wright, in all likelihood, was preparing his next, slim publication, *The Creative Will: Studies in the Philosophy and the Syntax of Aesthetics*, which was to appear in 1916. Leo Stein, meanwhile, though not yet actually working on his *A-B-C of Aesthetics*, which was to be published some twelve years later, was constantly concerning himself with problems connected with this, his ultimate project. Partly to keep himself busy and possibly also to round out his meagre budget, Leo, as he wrote to his sister after a very long silence, had broken 'into authorship'.[44]

It was no accident that Leo's very first article should have been

35 Morgan Russell, *Synchromy in Purplish Blue*, 1913

devoted to Cézanne. On the one hand, he found that the painter was a popular topic in American art circles, and on the other, this was a subject on which he had something to say and around which many of his incessant and probing speculations had evolved. It is not surprising, therefore, that Leo did not merely speak of Cézanne but tied various considerations on art in general to this subject.

He concluded by writing:

With practice even people who are not artists can learn to see so as to become conscious of a thing's reality. . . . In painting no one has dealt so powerfully with the rendering of some aspects of reality as Cézanne. . . . Cézanne gave no thought to the light in which things floated, but fixed his mind upon the solid thing itself. He tried to get, above all else, substantiality, finality, the eternal, the secure.

There is an obvious opposition between the character of Cézanne's work and the man's character, but there is no contradiction. A genuinely creative artist sees the world not as he is taught to see it, but freshly, in the light of his own needs. Cézanne, tormented, agitated, a prey to endless fears, with nothing in the world around him to sustain him, created for himself the thing he needed. Not, of course, the whole of it, for his ideal far outstripped his powers. His longing went out to a world not only solidly but joyously and conqueringly alive.

There is no painter of our time so pedestalled as Cézanne. Some hold him quite the greatest of all painters, and give their reasons why he should be so regarded. Those persons who decry him utterly can be neglected because their failure to see anything of worth in him does not refute what others see. It is absurd to say that he lacks beauty. No form that reaches organization can fail of that, and Cézanne's form is so effectively built up with color, cleanly, delicately and firmly welded, and through his best work run reverberant rhythms, that one who feels all this can sympathize with his extremest advocates. He is perhaps the most important figure in the history of modern painting, because of his elaboration of constructive color – color, that is, which models form. This was his legacy and made him a precursor. Most of the important painters immediately after him felt this great influence, and perhaps the most serious of the many faults of cubism and kindred movements is that they have diverted painting from this vital trend.

Against the splendid mastery of organized matter we must, however, place the limitations of Cézanne's effective interest. . . . And if we compare the range of life experience set forth by Cézanne with what the greatest masters have expressed, we see how narrow is that range. When one thinks of Giotto,

36 Stanton Macdonald-Wright, *'Conception'. Synchromy*, 1915

Rubens or Giorgione, of Titian, Renoir, Delacroix, and Michelangelo, presenting in substantial form so much of their passionate interest in nature, life and love, the field of Cézanne's interest is seen as something almost painfully restricted. He himself knew these limitations and bitterly regretted them. . . . He did a limited thing, but one so fundamental – he realized so splendidly the beauty and power of sheer substance – that those who can for the time being dispense with other elements of satisfaction find in him a source of illimitable content.[45]

Leo continued to write. In March 1918, he published an article on Renoir and the Impressionists.[46] This subject entailed, of course, a short discussion of Cézanne, though this time Leo's words appear written not so much with restraint, as with a total lack of enthusiasm. Cézanne no longer seemed to be the focal point of his artistic concepts; in the unavoidable comparison with Renoir, it was to the latter that Leo's preference went.

This was where the paths of Willard Huntington Wright and Leo Stein crossed once more. When Wright had compared the two painters in his *Modern Painting*, he had explained why, despite his admiration for Renoir, he considered Cézanne the greater painter. 'In Cézanne', Wright stated, 'the importance of parts is entirely submerged in the effect of the whole. Here is the main difference between these two great men: we enjoy each part of Renoir and are conducted by line to a completion; in Cézanne we are struck simultaneously by each interrelated part.' And he concluded, 'Cézanne, judged either as a theorist or as an achiever, is the pre-eminent figure in modern art. Renoir alone approaches his stature. Purely as a painter he is the greatest the world has produced. In the visual arts he is surpassed only by El Greco, Michelangelo and Rubens.'[47] In his article on Renoir and the Impressionists Leo did not allude to Wright's views on the artist, nor did he show any of Wright's perceptiveness when he discussed the various Impressionists. This time Leo chose not to acknowledge any awareness of the writings and ideas of one of the few authors who, like himself, was profoundly concerned with aesthetic problems.

In the course of the article, however, Leo devoted a lengthy portion to Cézanne, 'that strange man secluded in the south, at Aix in Provence, who with eager passion sought to make reality more real, to make into a picture the very substance of God's word', as he put it.

No greater contrast to Cézanne could be found than Renoir, the last of this illustrious group to come to recognition, and in whom the blend of the romantic with the realist is almost perfect. Whereas Cézanne was always painting on tomorrow's picture with passionate aspiration, Renoir with equally passionate joy was busy with today's. Whereas Cézanne despised even his best, Renoir enjoyed all that he did when he was in the right mood, and he was almost always in the right mood.

And Stein concluded this fairly trite comparison with the words, 'Cézanne cared for nothing but his soul's purpose and his soul's salvation, while Renoir finds his soul wherever he looks abroad.'[48]

By December 1919, Leo was back in Florence. The war having greatly reduced his modest financial reserves, he wrote the following year to Barnes to ask for his counsel concerning the disposal of what was left from his Paris collection: several Renoirs (among them various 'small and slight' ones) and 'some things, a Delacroix, Cézanne water colors, a Daumier, a Cézanne painting, and a bronze of Matisse.'[49]

It would seem that Leo had sold his green landscape by Cézanne to Barnes in 1913, at the time of his separation from his sister, to finance his move to Florence. The next year he had disposed of two paintings by Matisse in Germany, and little by little other works had followed, among them a number of Renoirs, up to Barnes' purchase of the *Bathers* by Cézanne soon after Leo's arrival in America. Now Leo shipped to New York a number of the works listed in his letter to Barnes, who rejected the Renoirs as too sketchy and insignificant – it is true that by then he owned a great number of paintings by the artist, among which mediocre works were already well represented. On the other hand, it was somewhat cruel of Barnes also to refuse the small Cézanne painting of apples, now that Leo was in need. This powerfully constructed composition was certainly just as fine, if not actually better, than a related still-life that Barnes had acquired at the Rouart sale back in 1912. Durand-Ruel purchased the small canvas – which Leo had once described to his sister as having 'a unique importance to me that nothing can replace'[50] – for $800.

Leo was now left without a single work by Cézanne and possibly also by Renoir, but then he was constantly moving away from what had at one time been of paramount and life-enhancing importance to him. When Leo now spoke of the green landscape that had been his first purchase of a work by Cézanne, he sounded surprisingly uninspired and indifferent. His words were as flat and repetitious as many of his sister's monotonous statements (which he hated). 'The composition is a good one', he wrote, 'and the space handling for the most part even exceptionally good. It was altogether a good beginning.'[51] And that was all he found to say on the very picture that had launched him on his career as the most eclectic and discerning collector of modern art in those distant days! It is a fact, however, that this prodigious career had been a very short-lived one, and that Leo had soon tired of Matisse, of Picasso as he turned to Cubism and now, to a certain extent, even of Cézanne. When in 1945, two years before his death, he again saw the pictures that once belonged to Loeser, which had been such a revelation to him in 1904, he wrote to a friend that in this group 'a little figure composition is charming and there is one fine olive tree landscape.'[52] Yet there were several infinitely more imposing works in the collection. What had happened was that Leo – cured of his neuroses? – had lost his capacity for enthusiasm. He himself must have been aware of this, for in another comment on the Loeser collection he said (possibly with a tinge of regret): 'The pictures are about as they were, but I am not, and only one or two still seemed to me important.'[53]

Cézanne was no longer an essential peg in Leo's aesthetic system, yet to give him up was to break with a relatively happy phase of his past. Step by step, he nevertheless detached himself from Cézanne, and this detachment eventually almost turned into contempt. As Cézanne's art was ever more widely acclaimed, Leo Stein, one of the very first to have recognized its crucial significance, actually tried to reverse his position. His negative attitude was first expressed openly in an article on Picasso which he wrote in 1924 for the *New Republic*. It offered him an opportunity to vent his bitterness over the evolution of the artist whom he could not forgive his Cubist phase, long passed, but who also seemed unable to please him with any of his succeeding styles, even his

56

37 *Woodland*, 1890–92

drawings. It was as though he had to take revenge for once having admired Picasso without foreseeing that Picasso would develop in directions of which he, Leo, would not approve. But while he thus, in a way, settled an old account with the painter for having disappointed him, Leo also availed himself of the occasion to speak of his steadily increasing disaffection with Cézanne. It was of course easy to link Picasso with Cézanne, and this he proceeded to do, writing:

The group of artists in which Picasso found himself [in the Rue Ravignan days in Paris] was feeling more and more strongly the influence of Cézanne and tending more and more to regard as an end what to Cézanne had been a means

– substantial form. Cézanne's personal ideal had two poles: to make of impressionism something solid like Poussin, and to do over Poussin in impressionistic terms. His ideal, that is, was of a complete pictorial art. In fact, he rarely got as far as this, and was entangled to the end in the problem of means. Much of his work makes on me the painful impression as of a man tied up in a knot who is trying to undo himself. However, his concern with an essential problem, that of adequate expression in modern terms, made him the chief of the modern clan.[54]

After his 1924 article on Picasso with its disturbing image of Cézanne, the prolific expounder completed the sorry evolution that led him from the concept of 'Cézanne and I' to the much less rewarding one of 'I and Cézanne'. When he eventually summed up his position, he wrote:

There was a moment when Cézanne brought something fresh which I assimilated with great enthusiasm and joy. What Cézanne gave was important but his own expression of it was limited, constrained, and in many ways extremely insufficient, and when I had made the assimilation I found very little of him left over that was endurable. For a while, no painter excited my interest more vitally. Now no pictures interest me less. He is for me more completely the squeezed lemon than any other artist of anything like equal importance.[55]

Thus taking leave from Cézanne, it was Leo Stein who gave 'the painful impression as of a man tied up in a knot who is trying to undo himself.'

NOTES

1 Irene Gordon, *Four Americans in Paris* (New York: Museum of Modern Art, 1970), p. 13. Gertrude died in 1946.

2 Ibid, p. 22.

3 See Leo Stein, *Appreciation: Painting, Poetry and Prose* (New York: Crown, 1947), p. 154; also Leo Stein, *Journey into the Self: Being the Letters, Papers & Journals of Leo Stein,*, ed. Edmund Fuller (New York: Crown, 1950), p. 204. Stein first met Berenson in Florence in the spring of 1896; see Hutchins Hapgood, *A Victorian in the Modern World* (New York: Harcourt, Brace, 1939), p. 59.

4 Stein, *Appreciation*, op. cit., pp. 155–56.

5 Gertrude and Leo Stein to Mabel Weeks, Paris, n.d.; Beinecke Rare Book and Manuscript Library, Yale University. This document was brought to my attention by Irene Gordon who, on internal evidence, dates it to November 1904.

6 A tentative list of works by Cézanne owned by Leo and Gertrude was established by Margaret Potter in 1969–70 during her research on their collection and that of their brother and sister-in-law, Michael and Sarah Stein, for the exhibition held at the Museum of Modern Art, New York, 1970–71, under the title *Four Americans in Paris*, which she directed.

7 Fernande Olivier, *Picasso et ses amis* (Paris: Stock, 1923), p. 102.

8 It was obviously to Michael and Sally Stein's home rather than to Leo and Gertrude's that C. Lewis Hind referred when he wrote: 'There's a large white room in Paris, in a private house, hung almost entirely with paintings by Matisse. Students, disciples, and dilettanti gather there on Saturday evenings. Strangers come. The many are indignant; the few begin by being uneasy and end in fetters.'

C. Lewis Hind, *The Consolations of a Critic* (London: Adam and Charles Black), 1911, p. 81.

9 It was Elizabeth McCausland, in her book on *A. H. Maurer* (New York: A. A. Wyn, 1951, p. 83), who first mentioned that the two Russians had been friendly with the Steins. Her dating of the acquaintance at 'about 1905 or 1906' may be accurate for Shchukin but is probably a little too early for Morosov. On the other hand, a recently published account, according to which Shchukin was encouraged by Durand-Ruel to take an interest in Picasso, appears to be without any basis; see *Paris-Moscou, 1900–1930* (exhibition catalogue), Centre National Georges Pompidou, Paris, May–November 1979, p. 26.

10 Alfred Maurer to Leo Stein, Paris, 2 August 1905; quoted by McCausland in *A. H. Maurer*, op. cit., p. 89.

11 See Gertrude Stein, 'Gertrude Stein in Paris, 1903–1907', in *The Autobiography of Alice B. Toklas* (London: John Lane, The Bodley Head, 1933), p. 12.

12 Mabel Dodge Luhan, *Intimate Memoirs*, vol. 2 ('European Experiences'), (New York: Harcourt, Brace, 1935), pp. 322, 321.

13 Leo Stein to Mabel Weeks, Paris, n.d.; in Leo Stein, *Journey*, op. cit., pp. 15–16. Irene Gordon, whose transcription of the original letter in the Beinecke Rare Book and Manuscript Library, Yale University, is given here, dates it on internal evidence to early 1905 (possibly January or February).

14 Stein, *Appreciation*, op. cit., pp. 200, 201.

15 Ibid., p. 84.

16 Leo Stein to Mabel Weeks, Paris, 15 February 1910; Beinecke Rare Book and

Manuscript Library, Yale University. This document was brought to my attention by Irene Gordon.

17 On Berenson's acquaintance with Picasso, see Bernard Berenson, *Sketch for a Self-portrait* (New York: Pantheon, 1949), p. 46. On his meeting with Matisse, see his letter to his wife, Paris, 9 October 1908, quoted in *The Bernard Berenson Treasury*, ed. Hanna Kiel (New York, Simon and Schuster, 1962), p. 136.

18 Berenson, *Sketch*, op. cit., pp. 44–45. It was an unsigned review of the 1908 Salon d'Automne in *The Nation* on 29 October 1908, containing a contemptuous remark concerning Matisse, that prompted Berenson to write a letter to the Editor which appeared on 11 November; see Alfred H. Barr, Jr, *Matisse: His Art and His Public* (New York: Museum of Modern Art, 1951), pp. 111–12, 114.

19 Bernard Berenson to Mary Berenson, Ravenna, 4 September 1910; unpublished document, courtesy Professor Ernest Samuels, Evanston, Ill.

20 Willard Huntington Wright, *Modern Painting* (New York and London: John Lane, 1915), p. 150.

21 Morgan Russell to Andrew Dasburg, Paris, late August 1908; quoted by Gail Levin in *Synchromism and American Color Abstraction, 1910–25* (New York: George Braziller, 1978), p. 12.

22 Andrew Dasburg to his wife, Paris, 24 April 1910; quoted by Gail Levin in 'Andrew Dasburg, Recollections of the Avant-Garde', *Arts Magazine*, June 1978, p. 126. Dasburg was so impressed with Cézanne's work that his biographer could state: 'His life as an artist can be divided neatly into two parts: before and after the day he encountered Cézanne's work in Paris in 1910.' Van Deren Coke, *Andrew Dasburg* (Albuquerque: University of New Mexico Press, 1979), p. 2.

23 Leo Stein to Morgan Russell, Fiesole, 26 June 1910; quoted by Levin in *Synchromism*, op. cit., p. 12.

24 See for example Maurice Sterne, *Shadow and Light*, ed. C. L. Mayerson (New

York: Harcourt, Brace & World, 1952), p. 43.

25 Max Raphael, *Aufbruch in die Gegenwart* (Frankfurt am Main and New York: Qumran, Campus Verlag, 1985), p. 17; originally published in 'Erinnerungen um Picasso' (1911), *Davoser Revue*, 6, no. 11, 15 August 1931.

26 Leo Stein, *The A-B-C of Aesthetics* (New York: Boni & Liveright, 1927), p. 86. The sentence begins 'Twenty years ago when I was especially obsessed....' This obviously points to the period around 1907.

27 Bernard Berenson, *Piero della Francesca or the Ineloquent in Art* (London: Chapman & Hall, 1954), pp. 6, 7.

28 Hutchins Hapgood, *A Victorian*, op. cit., p. 131.

29 Gertrude Stein, *Lectures in America* (New York: Random House, 1935), quoted in *Pictures for a Picture of Gertrude Stein as a Collector and Writer on Art and Artists* (exhibition catalogue), Yale University Gallery, New Haven, 11 February–11 March 1951, p. 21.

30 Leo Stein is said to have felt that the artist's failure to rework the portrait around the newly introduced face left the painting stylistically incoherent. When friends complained to Picasso that Gertrude did not look at all like his painting, he was in the habit of shrugging his shoulders and saying: 'She will.' See James R. Mellow, *Charmed Circle – Gertrude Stein & Company* (New York and Washington DC; Praeger, 1974), p. 93.

31 Clive Bell, 'Paris in the 'Twenties', in *Old Friends* (London: Chatto & Windus, 1956), p. 173.

32 Stein, *Appreciation*, op. cit., pp. 166, 201.

33 See Janet Hobhouse, *Everybody Who Was Anybody: A Biography of Gertrude Stein* (London: Weidenfeld & Nicolson, 1975), pp. 77–78.

34 See Lamont Moore, preface in *Pictures for a Picture of Gertrude Stein*, op. cit., p. 15.

35 Gertrude Stein, preface in catalogue for Riba-Rovira exhibition, Galerie Roquepine, Paris, 1945, quoted by Moore,

op. cit., p. 18.

36 Among the Cézannes were the small still-life of apples (5), at least one of the two compositions of bathers (11), and their first purchase, the landscape (2), (unless the latter was sold to Barnes in 1913 in order to finance Leo's installation in Florence). On the division of the collection, see Leo's letter to his sister, Paris, n.d. [1913–14], *The Flowers of Friendship: Letters Written to Gertrude Stein*, ed. Donald Gallup (New York: Alfred A. Knopf, 1953), pp. 91–92.

37 Since there is no record of such a sale in the Bernheim-Jeune archives, Wright must have purchased these watercolours from Vollard, in whose ledgers his name also does not appear. What happened to these works is not known.

38 See William C. Agee and Barbara Rose, *Patrick Henry Bruce; American Modernist* (New York: Museum of Modern Art), 1979.

39 Tapes of Max Weber interviews (Columbia University, New York), vol. 1, p. 74. On Cézanne's *Bathers* that belonged to Matisse, see Alfred H. Barr, Jr, *Matisse*, op. cit., pp. 38–40.

40 On Matisse's *Académie*, see Alfred H. Barr, Jr *Matisse,* op. cit., pp. 116–18 and 550–52. See also Hélène Seckel, 'L'académie Matisse,' in *Paris–New York*, (exhibition catalogue), Paris, Centre National Georges Pompidou, June–September 1977, pp. 212–15.

On Cézanne's and especially Matisse's influence on American painters, see *The Advent of Modernism − Post-Impressionism and North American Art, 1900–1918*, ed. Peter Morris, Judith Zilczer, William C. Agee (exhibition catalogue), High Museum of Art, Atlanta, 1986.

41 Leo to Gertrude Stein, New York, 15 February 1916, in Leo Stein, *Journey*, op. cit., pp. 71–72.

42 Willard Huntington Wright, 'What is Modern Painting?', introductory essay in *The Forum Exhibition of Modern American Painters* (exhibition catalogue), Anderson Galleries, New York, 13–25 March 1916,

p. 23; reprinted in a facsimile edition by Arno Press, New York, 1968.

43 See Jerome Mellquist, *The Emergence of an American Art* (New York: Charles Scribner's Sons, 1942), pp. 211, 246.

44 Leo to Gertrude Stein, 15 February 1916, in Leo Stein, *Journey*, op. cit., p. 71.

45 Leo Stein, 'Cézanne', *New Republic*, 22 January 1916, pp. 297–98.

46 In *New Republic*, 30 March 1918, pp. 250–60. This article was brought to my attention by Irene Gordon.

47 Willard Huntington Wright, *Modern Painting: Its Tendency and Meaning* (London and New York: John Lane, 1915), pp. 157, 163.

48 Stein, 'Renoir and the Impressionists', op. cit., p. 260.

49 Leo Stein to Albert C. Barnes, Settignano, 8 March 1921, in Stein, *Journey*, op. cit., pp. 86–87.

50 Leo to Gertrude Stein, Paris, 27, rue de Fleurus, n.d., in Leo Stein, *Journey*, op. cit., p. 57.

51 Leo Stein, *Appreciation*, op. cit., p. 155.

52 Leo Stein to Maurice Sterne, Settignano, 29 June 1945, in Leo Stein, *Journey*, op. cit., p. 252.

53 Stein, *Appreciation*, op. cit., p. 156.

54 Leo Stein, 'Pablo Picasso', *New Republic*, 23 April 1924, p. 229. This article was brought to my attention by Irene Gordon.

55 Stein, *The A-B-C of Aesthetics*, op. cit., p. 267. The problem as to *when* Stein first alluded to Cézanne as a 'squeezed lemon' is an extremely thorny one. In his article on the artist of 1916 he still spoke with appreciation of the painter. It would seem that his total disenchantment with Cézanne only set in somewhat later, but this is not certain. Unfortunately, Walter Pach gives no date for a conversation with Picasso which he quotes in this connection in *Queer Thing, Painting* (New York–London: Harper & Brothers, 1938, p. 128): 'Questioning me once about a difficulty I had had with a certain critic, whom I will call L., he got the quotation from the latter which I had objected to: that Cézanne was of no more

use, a sort of "squeezed lemon," to be exact. "Well," said Picasso, "if Cézanne is a squeezed lemon, you may be sure that M. L. has never had a taste of the juice."'

Aline B. Saarinen in *The Proud Possessors* (New York: Random House, 1958, p. 192) places Leo's detachment from Cézanne around 1910. But this does not appear plausible since, towards the end of 1913, when Leo and Gertrude divided their collection between themselves, Leo was still absolutely adamant that he would not give up the small still-life of apples (5). He only sold it in 1921.

LIST OF ILLUSTRATIONS

All paintings are by Cézanne unless otherwise indicated

63

22 Michael and Sally Stein, Matisse, Allan Stein and Hans Purrmann at Michael and Sally Stein's apartment, *c.* 1908. The Baltimore Museum of Art, The Cone Archives.

23 Morgan Russell, *Three Apples*, 1910. Oil on cardboard, $9\frac{3}{4} \times 12\frac{1}{8}$ (24.8 × 32.7). Collection, The Museum of Modern Art, New York. Given anonymously.

24 Leo Stein at the rue de Fleurus apartment, *c.* 1906. The Baltimore Museum of Art, The Cone Archives.

25 Alice Toklas and Gertrude Stein in Leo and Gertrude's apartment, 1922. Photograph by Man Ray. The Baltimore Museum of Art: The Cone Collection, formed by Dr. Claribel Cone and Miss Etta Cone of Baltimore, Maryland. BMA 1950/85.1.

26 Paintings by Matisse, Renoir and Cézanne in Leo and Gertrude Stein's apartment. The Baltimore Museum of Art, The Cone Archives.

27 Pablo Picasso, *Gertrude Stein*, 1906. Oil on canvas, $39\frac{1}{4} \times 32$ (99.7 × 81.3). Metropolitan Museum of Art, New York (Bequest of Gertrude Stein, 1946).

28 Leo and Gertrude Stein's apartment, with paintings by Picasso, Matisse and Renoir. The Baltimore Museum of Art, The Cone Archives.

29 Alfred Maurer, *Still-life*, 1907–08. Oil on canvas, $21\frac{1}{2} \times 18$ (54.6 × 45.7). Courtesy Salander-O'Reilly Galleries, New York.

30 Alfred Maurer, *Fauve Landscape*. Oil on gesso board, $21\frac{3}{4} \times 18$ (55.2 × 45.7). Courtesy Salander-O'Reilly Galleries, New York.

31 Patrick Henry Bruce, *Still-life*, *c.* 1921–22. Oil on canvas, $35 \times 45\frac{3}{4}$ (88.9 × 116.2). Whitney Museum of American Art, New York (anonymous gift).

32 *Three Bathers*, 1876–77. Oil on canvas, $20\frac{1}{2} \times 21\frac{1}{2}$ (52 × 54.5). Musée de la Ville de Paris, Petit Palais, Paris (gift of Henri Matisse).

33 Morgan Russell, *Still-life with Bananas*, 1912–13. Oil on canvas, $16 \times 18\frac{1}{4}$ (40.6 × 46.3). Collection Mr and Mrs Henry M. Reed, Montclair, New Jersey.

34 Stanton Macdonald-Wright, *Still-life with Skull*, 1912. Oil on canvas, $13\frac{3}{8} \times 19\frac{1}{4}$ (39 × 48.9). Private collection.

35 Morgan Russell, *Synchromy in Purplish Blue*, 1913. Oil on canvas, mounted on cardboard, $13 \times 9\frac{5}{8}$ (33 × 24.4). Collection Mrs Harry Lewis Winston (Dr and Mrs. Barnett Malbin), New York.

36 Stanton Macdonald-Wright, *'Conception'. Synchromy*, 1915. Oil on canvas, 30×24 (76.2 × 61). Whitney Museum of American Art (gift of George F. Of).

37 *Woodland*, 1890–92. Oil on canvas, $28\frac{3}{4} \times 36\frac{1}{4}$ (73 × 92). National Gallery of Art, Washington DC (presented to the government of the United States in memory of Charles A. Loeser).